Enid Blyton's NODDY annual 1996

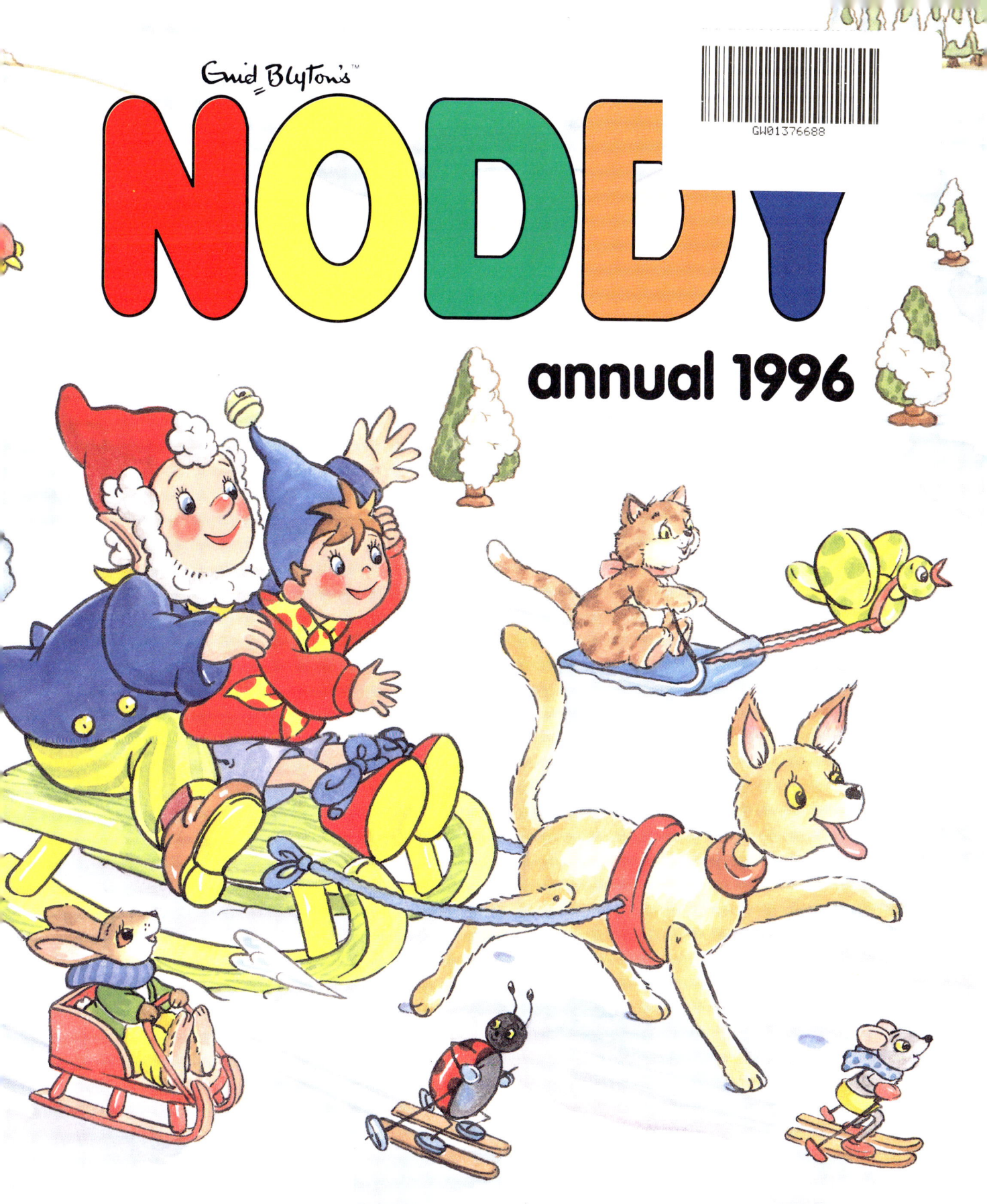

CONSULTANT EDITOR Gillian Baverstock   **EDUCATIONAL ADVISOR** Godfrey Hall
NEW ILLUSTRATIONS Andrew Geeson   **EDITOR** Jacqueline Russo

Original Text and Images copyright © Darrell Waters Ltd. 1949/68. Text and Images of BBC Television Series copyright © BBC Enterprises Ltd. 1992. Licensed by BBC Enterprises Ltd. All rights reserved.
Published in Great Britain by World International, an imprint of Egmont Publishing Ltd., Egmont House, PO Box 111, Great Ducie Street, Manchester M60 3BL.
Printed in Italy. ISBN 0 7498 2271 6
"NODDY" is a trademark of Darrell Waters Ltd., and is used under licence.
"Enid Blyton" (signature logotype) is a trademark of Darrell Waters Ltd., and is used under licence.

£4.99 UK only

CONTENTS

5 A letter from Noddy

6 Poem
Noddy's Car

7 Story
Noddy Goes Shopping

14 Toy Town School
– Learn about shops

16 Story
Noddy Loses His Money

18 Out with Mr Tubby
– In the Garden

20 Story
Noddy and the Milkman

24 Toy Town School
– Learn about helping

25 Puzzle
Dot-to-Dot

26 Story
Noddy is Very Funny

32 Toy Town School
– Learn about common sense

33 Puzzle
Noddy's Word Search

34 Story
The Two Bad Goblins

36 Out with Mr Tubby
Noddy makes a Christmas pudding for the birds

38 Story
Noddy and his bell

42 Toy Town School
Learn about sounds

44 Learn to Read with Noddy

45 Puzzle
Spot the Difference

46 Story
Noddy Goes to a Party

48 Toy Town School
Learn about cooking

50 Story
After the Party

57 Puzzle
Hide and Seek

58 Toy Town School
Learn about making mistakes

60 Colour in with Noddy

61 Poem
Lucky Little Noddy

62 Competition

TOY TOWN SCHOOL NOTE FOR GROWN-UPS
The "Toy Town School" pages have been designed to develop children's progress through the early stages of the National Curriculum.
Most activities lead towards Levels 1 and 2.

A Letter from Noddy

Hello, boys and girls!

I've had such a lot of adventures lately that I've put them into another Noddy Annual for you. I do wish you would come to Toy Town and share some of them with me.

If you want to visit me, you know where I live – in a dear little house of bricks, called 'House-for-One'. I live next door to Mr and Mrs Tubby Bear, and they are very kind to me.

Next to my house is a little garage for my car. It has a hooter that goes 'parp-parp!' whenever it sees the skittle family playing – or Mr Plod the policeman round the corner!

Sometimes I go to the wood to see my friend Big-Ears the Brownie. He lives in a toadstool house with his old cat, Whiskers, and he is very kind to me. I like having tea with him in his toadstool house.

I take my little red and yellow car out into the town every day, to see if I can pick up passengers who want to go here or there – perhaps to the station to catch the Toyland Train. I charge sixpence a time, though I often think that old Jumbo ought to pay two sixpences, he's so big.

If you ever come to find me in Toy Town, look out for someone in a red shirt, and a blue hat. My hat has a bell at the end of it, so you'll always hear me coming – jingle-jing, jingle-jing!

Now I must sign my name in my best handwriting.
Big-Ears sends you his love, and so do I.
Love from

Noddy

Noddy's Car

"Oh nobody knows
How nice it feels
To own a car
With four little wheels,

Headlights too,
And a bonnet bright
And two little doors
That fasten tight!

You hoot very loud,
You go along fine,
I feel very glad
Because you are mine!

Oh, dear little car
I really must say
You're the best little car
In Toyland today."

Noddy Goes Shopping

"It's time I went shopping," said little Noddy. So he took down his basket, got into his car and away he went.

"Parp-parp!" said Noddy's little car.

"Don't run across the road like that, Connie Kitten!" shouted Noddy.

The little car turned the corner, and hooted again, "Parp-parp!"

"Don't play cricket in the middle of the road!" shouted Noddy at three small teddy bears.

He came to the shops and got out. He parked his car in a safe corner, and then went to do his shopping.

"A jar of strawberry jam to have when Big-Ears comes to tea," he said to the shopkeeper. "And some polish for my car. Oh, and some cocoa because there isn't much left. And please put them all into my basket."

"The handle of your basket needs mending," said Mr Grocer Doll. "It looks as if it's going to break."

"Oh, dear – yes, Big-Ears did tell me to be sure and mend it last week," said Noddy, his head nodding as he remembered. "But I forgot. Never mind – I'll mend it tomorrow."

"That means it will *never* be mended!" said the grocer. "Do it today!"

Noddy went to the milk-shop next.

"A pint of milk, please," he said. "The milkman didn't leave me any this morning. He forgot all about me."

"I expect you were fast asleep when he called," said Miss Dairy Doll. "Goodness, Noddy – your basket handle is soon going to give way."

"Yes, I know," said Noddy. "But I'm carrying everything home in my car."

He went to the greengrocer's. "One large banana – a nice curly one, please," he said. "They taste better than the straight ones!"

"Look, Noddy – your basket needs mending," said the shopkeeper, putting in a very curly banana.

"I know, I know, I know!" said Noddy getting quite cross. "*Everybody* keeps telling me about it. I'm going to mend it tomorrow, I keep *telling* everybody that!"

He went off with his basket, which was now getting quite full. The sun shone down on him and he felt warm and happy.

He did a little dance as he went along, and the basket jerked in his hand.

"Here I go,
My shopping done,
I really have
A lot of fun!"
sang Noddy.

He jerked his basket again – and the handle broke! Everything fell out and rolled on to the pavement.

"There goes the milk – and the jam – and the polish!" groaned Noddy. "Come here, curly banana, don't bounce away like that!"

He picked everything up – but now that the handle of the basket was broken, the shopping was very difficult to carry. Then one side of the basket began to give way, where the handle had broken – and things began to slip out again.

"Oh, dear, oh, dear – why didn't I mend you, basket?" said Noddy. "There goes the cocoa tin again! Hey – stop rolling down the hill!"

Just at that moment all the Noah's Ark animals came by, walking two by two, very well-behaved indeed. How they laughed to see Noddy running after the cocoa tin, and dropping the tin of polish and the banana as he went!

Then he dropped the jar of strawberry jam, and it broke! Noddy stepped into the sticky mess, his foot slipped and he sat down in the jam!

The Noah's Ark animals laughed and laughed! The two bears laughed so much that they had to hold on to one another. Noddy was very, very angry.

"You unkind things! You very horrid animals! Why don't you help me, instead of laughing at me? I've got all my shopping to carry and my car is a long way away!"

The Noah's Ark animals went on their way, giggling and laughing – all except one. This was kind Katie Kangaroo.

"Noddy! I'll help you," she said. "Get up out of that sticky jam! Oh, my – what a mess you're in!"

"How can you help me?" asked Noddy, getting up. "Have you a basket? That's what I really want."

"No. But I've got a very big pocket," said Katie Kangaroo.

"A pocket? Where?" asked Noddy, in surprise. "I didn't know animals had pockets!"

"Kangaroos have," said Katie. "Look, I've a fine one. It's really meant to carry baby kangaroos, but I don't see why my pocket can't carry shopping."

"Oh! That's really a very good idea!" said Noddy, pleased. "Here – take this tin of cocoa, Katie Kangaroo – and this bottle of milk, and ..."

Well, Katie Kangaroo's pocket took everything comfortably and Noddy was very grateful to her. "Come along to my car," he said. "If you'll carry my shopping as far as that, I'll give you a ride home and we'll have some cocoa and biscuits – and then I'll drive you all the way back to the Ark."

"OH!" said Katie Kangaroo, and she jumped right over a wall and back again in delight. "OH! I've never been in a car in my life!"

"Please don't jump over walls when you've got my shopping in your pocket," said Noddy, in alarm. "KATIE! Did you hear me – you've jumped over that wall again and the bottle of milk nearly flew out!"

"I can't help it!" said Katie, looking as if she was going to jump over a house next. "I feel so excited to be going riding in a car, Noddy!"

Noddy took her paw very firmly and led her to where he had parked his car. She carried his shopping very well in her pocket, and felt proud when they met Mr and Mrs Toy Dog, who stared in surprise.

"Get into the car carefully," said Noddy. "Don't jump in, Katie. Oh, dear – what a jumpy person you are. Now here we go!"

And off they went, and Katie Kangaroo screamed in delight. "Oh, it's lovely! Oh, I do like it! Oh, Noddy, please let me drive!"

"Certainly not," said Noddy, shocked. "Oh look – we've caught up with all the Noah's Ark animals, Katie. Now, sit up straight and behave yourself."

And, to Mr Noah's amazement, and all the animals' surprise, Noddy's car drove by them, hooting loudly – and there was Katie Kangaroo sitting beside Noddy, waving to them very grandly.

"Now how did Katie Kangaroo get there?" said Mr Noah. "What a very peculiar thing!"

Katie really did enjoy herself. She had a cup of cocoa and two biscuits at Noddy's little

House-For-One, and then Noddy drove her back to the Ark.

"Thank you very much, Noddy," she said, as she got out of the car, watched by all the other animals, who were looking out of the windows in surprise. "And don't forget – if you want to borrow my pocket for shopping, just let me know – and I'll lend it to you with pleasure."

"Thank you, Katie," said Noddy. "But the trouble is – I'd have to borrow you too!"

Off he went home again, wishing and wishing that he hadn't put off mending his basket.

"I've got three things to do now," he told his little car. "I've got to wash my jammy shorts, I've got to wash the driving-seat where I've been sitting because there's jam there now too, and I simply *must* mend my shopping basket."

"Parp-parp," said the car, and Noddy knew quite well what it was saying!

"Well, Noddy – go and do it *now*!"

Noddy Says!

- What shops did Noddy visit?
- What did the different shopkeepers say to Noddy?
- What happened to Noddy's shopping?
- How did Katie Kangaroo help Noddy with his shopping?

Toy Town School
with Miss Prim

Learn about shops

Something to know

In the story 'Noddy Goes Shopping', Noddy goes round the village buying all the things on his list. There are lots of different shops that only sell certain things. Greengrocers sell vegetables and fruit and a baker sells bread and cakes. Some supermarkets and village shops sell everything from bread to bananas.

Something to understand

Many of the things we buy in the shops come from other countries. Oranges and bananas come from hot countries. Some vegetables come from Africa and America. Because it is important that they are fresh when they arrive, they are put on planes so that they will get here quickly. Have a look at the labels of some of the tins and packets and see where they have come from.

Something to do

Noddy has to get some shopping for Big-Ears. Which shops will he have to visit?

2 oranges

a loaf of bread

a stamp

a packet of fruit gums

a book

bookshop,   greengrocer,   baker,   Post Office,   sweet shop

Something to make

You will need

a small cardboard box
a strip of card
water based paints
glue
paintbrush
pot

Find a small cardboard box.
Ask a grown-up to help cut out a strip of card.
Stick the card on to the box so that the handle is firm.
Decorate the outside of your shopping basket using the paints.

Get some empty packets and put them inside the basket. See if you can find out what was inside the packets and how much the things cost.

The next time you are in the supermarket ask if you can help put the different things into the trolley or basket.

MISS PRIM'S NOTE FOR GROWN-UPS

It is a good idea to involve your child when you next go shopping. Get them to help select items and put them into your basket. Discuss with them where some of the things have come from and why it is important to keep some of them cold whilst they are in the shop.

Noddy Loses His Money

1 It was raining, so Noddy borrowed Big-Ears' umbrella.

2 He left his car behind and went shopping all by himself.

3 He put the umbrella down when he went into the grocer's.

4 He took out his purse – but oh, dear, all the money fell out!

5 He could not find it anywhere. He could not buy anything.

6 He went sadly out of the shop, and met dear old Big-Ears.

7 "Now I can have my umbrella!" said Big-Ears, very pleased.

8 He put it up – and good gracious – what a shower of money!

9 "My money fell inside the umbrella – and I didn't know!" cried Noddy.

17

Out with Mr Tubby

"It's a frosty morning!" shivers Noddy. We look at the bare garden where we have cut down the dead plants. "There are no flowers for the bees or the butterflies ," says Noddy. "And my bulbs won't grow until spring comes."

We watch the beech tree's golden leaves and the brown leaves of the oak beginning to fall. "Soon only the evergreen trees will have leaves left," Noddy says.

"The swallows flew to warmer countries weeks ago," says Mr Tubby. "Now, we'll watch for the redwings arriving . They can find more food here than in their snowy lands."

"I know frogs sleep upside down in the muddy bottom of the pond," says Noddy. "What do worms do ?" We search the lawn and find leaves pulled into the wormholes. "The worms sleep underground and they are keeping their burrows warm," Mr Tubby answers.

"The hedgehog is fast asleep in a cosy hole," says Mr Tubby. "The squirrel is hiding nuts to nibble on a sunny winter's day."

Bumpy dog bounds up . He is growing his thick furry winter coat. "I must go and look out my warm winter clothes too!" laughs Noddy.

Tick these pictures as you see the things during the year.

beech leaf		redwing		worm	
oak leaf		bumble bee		hedgehog	
fir twig		red admiral butterfly		squirrel	
swallow		frog		dog	

Noddy and the Milkman

This morning, naughty Bumpy Dog knocks Mr Milko over. Poor Mr Milko is very surprised but luckily Noddy catches the milk. "You are a very bad dog, Bumpy!" shouts Noddy.

"I can't deliver my milk today because I've got to visit my sick brother," says Mr Milko.

"I'll deliver it for you," Noddy says. Here he is putting it in the back of his car.

Noddy delivers the milk to Miss Pink Cat. He is about to take the empty bottles when Bumpy Dog comes running up. He is so pleased to see Noddy that he knocks the bottles over.

The milk bottles roll away down the road with Bumpy after them. Noddy chases Bumpy to the garage. "Stop Bumpy!" he shouts to Mr Sparks. Bumpy leaps on Mr Sparks' trolley and away he goes.

Bumpy Dog is enjoying himself. He races through Toy Town nearly knocking over Mr Wobbly Man, Clockwork Mouse and Mr Plod. "Stop, Bumpy Dog!" shouts Mr Plod, angrily. But Bumpy can't stop!

Finally, Bumpy crashes into Dinah Doll's stall. Noddy, together with Mr Tubby Bear, is still chasing him. "Catch Bumpy!" yells Noddy to Dinah Doll. Clever Dinah! She gives Bumpy a bone and he sits down.

Mr Tubby takes Bumpy home and Noddy goes on with his milk round. At the police station the two goblins are in prison. "Two extra pints today, Noddy," says Mr Plod. "Here are two extra pennies for you."

When Noddy meets Mr Milko at the station, he gives him the milk money and the two extra pennies. "Thank you, Noddy," says Mr Milko. "I must ring your little bell, I am so pleased!"

Toy Town School
with Miss Prim

Learn about helping

Something to know

In the story 'Noddy and the Milkman', Mr Milko has the job of delivering everyone's milk. He collects the milk in bottles from the dairy early every morning. His customers have to leave their clean empty bottles by the front door so they can be returned to the dairy, cleaned and used again.

Something to understand

When Mr Milko has to visit his sick brother, Noddy helps him by delivering his milk. Helping people in trouble is very important. Can you think of any times when you needed help? Who helped you – mum, dad, your teacher, a friend? What can you do to help your family or friends?

MISS PRIM'S NOTE FOR GROWN-UPS

Can your child think of ways of helping people? Who might help your child? This might be an opportunity to stress the importance of not going off with a stranger.

Something to do

Can you help Mr Milko deliver his milk bottles? Draw the right number by each house.

3

1

2

1

1

Dot-to-Dot

Mr Milko is visiting his sick brother so Noddy is delivering his milk for him. Join the dots to see who wants two pints of milk today.

Noddy is Very Funny

Next door to Noddy lived Mr and Mrs Tubby Bear. Mrs Tubby was always very kind to Noddy, and sometimes made him currant buns, and washed his curtains for him.

And sometimes Noddy was kind to Mrs Tubby too, and did odd jobs for her. He would knock at her door and say, "Mrs Tubby, can I do anything for you today?" And there was usually something Mrs Tubby wanted him to do.

One day she called to him. "Little Noddy! The farmer has promised to give me a good hen to lay me eggs for breakfast. Do you think you could go and fetch it for me?"

So off went Noddy at once. "The hen is in that barn," said the farmer. "You can go and fetch her yourself."

So Noddy went to get the hen. It took him a long time to catch her. "How do you take a squirming hen home?" wondered little Noddy. "I'll make her walk in front of me, just like the farmer with his cows!"

He shooed the hen out of the barn, and shouted to it. "Walk in front of me!" But the hen wouldn't. It ran away at top speed, clucking. Noddy spent the whole morning trying to make it walk home in front of him. In the end it mixed itself up with all the other hens and Noddy didn't know which was which.

He went home and told Mrs Tubby. She laughed. "Silly Noddy! You should have tucked the hen comfortably under your arm and held her there. That's the way to do it!"

"I'll do that next time," said Noddy. So when Mrs Tubby asked him to go and get some ice-cream for her tea-party, he knew what to do! He bought the ice-cream, and tucked it well under his arm.

But dear me, it was a very hot day, and soon the ice-cream melted. It dropped all down his coat and his shorts, and made a terrible mess behind him as he walked.

"Oh, dear, Mrs Tubby, the ice-cream's all melted!" said poor Noddy, when he got back. Mrs Tubby shook her head at him.

"Oh, Noddy, Noddy! You should have taken a basket and put it safely in there. That's the way to do it!"

Well, it wasn't long before Mrs Tubby asked him to go and fetch her sister's little dog for her. "He's coming here for a bit," she said, "while my sister is away. Fetch him for me, there's a dear, Noddy!"

So Noddy went to fetch the dog, and he remembered what Mrs Tubby had said about his shopping last time, and he took a basket.

But do you suppose the dog would stay in Noddy's basket? Not a bit of it! He kept jumping out, and poor Noddy kept chasing him and putting him back. He was very hot and bothered when he got home.

Mrs Tubby was surprised to see the dog lying uncomfortably in the basket. "He's so heavy, and so naughty," panted Noddy. "He just *wouldn't* stay in the basket!"

"Little Noddy, I sometimes wonder where you keep your brains," said Mrs Tubby.

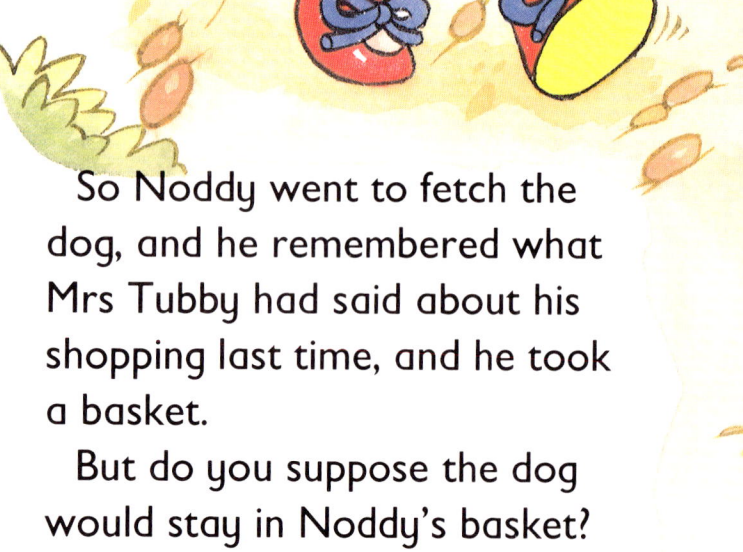

"I didn't know I had any," said Noddy, surprised. "Mrs Tubby, what *should* I have done to bring the dog home properly, please?"

"You should have tied a string to him and made him follow you," said Mrs Tubby. "He might have dragged behind a bit, but he would have had to come with you. That's the way to do it!"

"I'll remember next time," said Noddy, and gave the dog a pat.

Now the next time Mrs Tubby wanted him to help her, she asked him to go to the fish-shop and fetch some herrings for breakfast. Noddy set off at once. He took a long piece of string with him, because he remembered what Mrs Tubby had said to him last time.

The fishmonger chose him some nice herrings. "Brought any paper to wrap them in?" he asked. "And where's your basket?"

"I don't need paper," said Noddy. "I've got some string," and he took the herrings. He tied the string tightly round them, and then threw the herrings on the ground. "Come along, herrings," he said. "We're going back to Mrs Tubby's!"

And back they went, Noddy first, and the herrings dragging behind on the string. Noddy felt pleased with himself at first. But soon he looked round in fright.

A cat was running behind, sniffing at the herrings in surprise and delight. Herrings! On a string! She pounced on them and took a bite.

"Don't do that!" said Noddy crossly, and he jerked the herrings away.

"Mee-ow," said the cat, loudly, as she ran behind. "MEE-OW!" All the cats nearby heard her, and they smelt the herrings too and came running. When Noddy looked behind to see why the herrings kept stopping, he was full of astonishment. Seven cats ran behind him, having nibbles at the herrings whenever they could! By the time he got back to Mrs Tubby there wasn't a scrap of herring left!

"Silly little Noddy!" said Mrs Tubby. "You should have had the fish well wrapped up in sheets of newspaper and carried them. That's the way to do it."

So next time Mrs Tubby sent him on an errand Noddy took some sheets of newspaper with him. He had to go and fetch Mr Tubby's pet rabbit from a friend's.

When he tried to wrap it up in the newspaper the rabbit was scared. It leapt straight out of Noddy's hands, kicked away the newspaper, and ran for its life!

Poor Noddy went home crying. "The rabbit's gone, Mrs Tubby," he wept. "It's lost. It wouldn't let me wrap it up!"

"Now don't cry, little Noddy," said Mrs Tubby. "Look out into the garden! The rabbit came straight back here, and it's quite safe and happy. I don't think I will let you do any more errands until you have grown a few brains."

"I'll grow some," said Noddy, smiling and nodding his head. "I really will!"

And he really would, if only he knew how to!

Toy Town School
with Miss Prim

Something to know

In the story 'Noddy is Very Funny', Noddy is asked by Mrs Tubby Bear to do some jobs for her. But when he goes to do them he forgets to use his common sense. He tucks the ice-cream under his arm and puts Mrs Tubby Bear's sister's dog in a basket instead of putting it on a piece of string. Not using his common sense meant that Noddy got into a real mess.

Something to understand

It is always important that you think carefully about what you do and use your common sense, otherwise you might get into trouble or have an accident. Don't touch things that are hot and always stop, look both ways and make sure that the road is clear before you cross. Never go with strangers.

Think whether what you are doing is right or wrong and what might happen if you do the wrong thing.

Something to do

Look at the things below which have been drawn from above. Match the words and the pictures.

pond

tree

boat

house

teapot

MISS PRIM'S NOTE FOR GROWN-UPS

Get your child to use their common sense to work out what the drawings might be. Draw some more examples and see if they can work out what they are. Discuss with them the importance of using your common sense. Give them a variety of different situations and ask them what they might do. These could include what should they do if approached by a stranger. Talking with your child is a very important part of language development.

Noddy's Word Search

Noddy is going shopping. Can you find all the things on his shopping list in the word square? The words are in straight lines which may appear across or down. You can use the letters more than once.

Shopping List
- milk
- cakes
- eggs
- sugar
- tea
- cheese
- biscuits
- apples
- oranges
- butter

t	e	a	w	a	q	c	w	r	s
n	l	p	t	o	c	a	k	e	s
e	c	h	e	e	s	e	b	f	b
g	r	q	b	c	o	e	i	m	u
g	h	j	m	k	r	d	s	i	t
s	u	g	a	r	a	f	c	l	t
z	t	e	c	v	n	j	u	k	e
r	l	i	k	x	g	l	i	o	r
o	q	w	p	v	e	a	t	g	z
a	p	p	l	e	s	l	s	w	d

The Two Bad Goblins

1 One morning the Bumpy Dog was caught by two Red goblins.

2 They tied a note round his neck. "Go to Noddy!" they said.

3 He found Noddy and Big-Ears. "A note from Tessie," said Noddy.

4 "She wants us to meet her in the wood." Big-Ears was puzzled.

5 "It's not Tessie's writing, but the goblins! Fetch Mr Plod!" cried Noddy.

34

6 They told Mr Plod, and he and Big-Ears set off on bicycles.

7 In the wood they saw the goblins leap out to steal Noddy's car.

8 But Mr Plod and Big-Ears caught them – oh, what a shock!

9 Away they went to the police station in Noddy's little car!

Out with Mr Tubby

"The birds look so cold in the snow," says Noddy. "I wish we could give them a Christmas treat." Mr Tubby thinks for a little while. "Well, we could give them a Christmas tree and a Christmas pudding. Mrs Tubby will help us!"

Next morning, Noddy drives to Toy Town. He buys 250 grammes of wild bird seed, 3 sprays of millet, and 250 grammes of peanuts in their shells. Then he chooses a little Christmas tree in a pot.

Noddy shells some of the peanuts and threads the rest of the peanuts into necklaces. He puts a loop of thread through some little biscuits from Mrs Tubby and ties thread round pieces of coconut from Mr Tubby. Now he's ready to decorate the little tree.

First, he puts mistletoe berries at the top. He arranges the peanut necklaces around the tree and hangs the biscuits and pieces of coconut from the branches with some holly berries. He ties each millet spray to the tree with red ribbon. Mrs Tubby gives him some silver tinsel and Noddy proudly puts the pretty little tree outside.

Next, Mrs Tubby helps him make the birds' Christmas pudding. She chops up the peanuts and puts them in a bowl. Noddy adds the birdseed and a handful of currants. Mr Tubby brings in some dried sunflower seeds. Noddy mixes everything well while Mrs Tubby melts some dripping on her stove. She pours it carefully over the mixture, stirs it, and leaves it to cool.

When the pudding is cold Noddy cuts a thick slice and puts it by his Christmas tree. Then he and Mr and Mrs Tubby Bear watch through the window as all the birds fly down excitedly.

These are some of the birds who visited the Christmas tree and tasted the Christmas pudding. Watch the birds yourself and tick each picture as you see each bird. Try to learn the name of each one.

Robin

Blackbird

Thrush

Great tit

Blue tit

Sparrow

Wren

Starling

Chaffinch

Noddy and his Bell

One morning Mr Plod came to visit Noddy. "A burglar went to Sally Skittle's house last night and stole some food," said Mr Plod sternly.

"I was in bed then," said Noddy. "Anyway I wouldn't go out stealing!"

"Sally Skittle heard your bell ringing so it must have been you," said Mr Plod sternly.

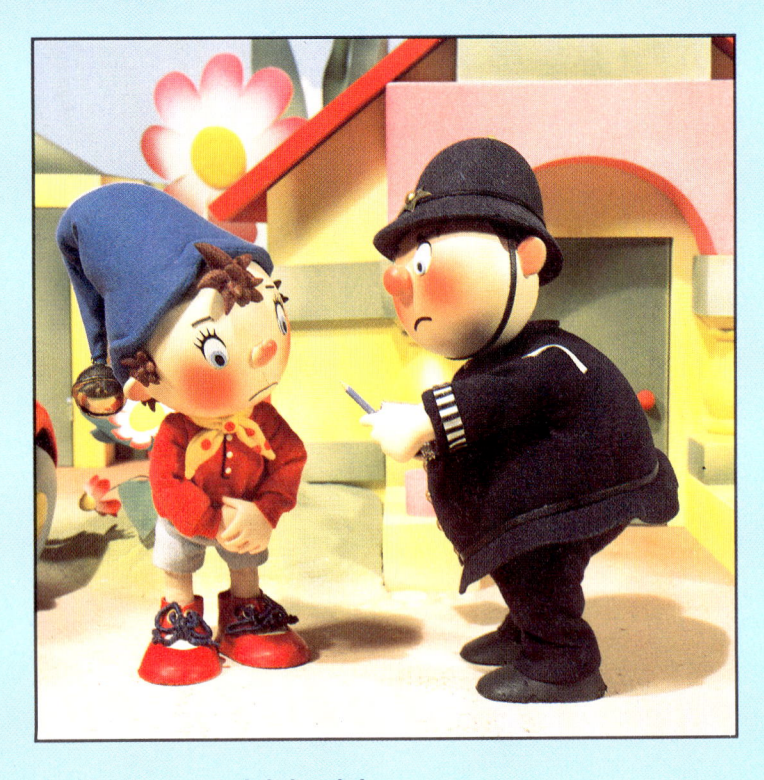

"It wasn't, it wasn't, it wasn't," shouted Noddy.

Poor Noddy! When he went into Toy Town that day, no one would talk to him. No one would drive in his car. Everyone was talking about the thief with the jingling bell who had stolen some jam tarts, a meat pie and a chocolate cake from Sally Skittle. They all thought the thief must have been Noddy.

Noddy tried to talk to Mr Wobbly Man but he wobbled quickly off down the street. Mr Jumbo hurried past him without speaking. Mr Sparks at the Garage pushed himself under a car and stayed there. Noddy drove sadly home wondering what he could do. He went into his little house with big tears rolling down his cheeks.

"Nobody likes me any more," wept Noddy, sitting on his stool. "I'm all alone!"

"No you're not, Noddy!" said a little voice. Tessie Bear had come to find him. "I know you're not a thief. We'll have to find out who the real thief is."

"But how can we?" asked Noddy, cheering up a little.

"I've got an idea," said Tessie.

Tessie took Noddy down to Dinah Doll's stall and asked her if anyone had bought a bell like Noddy's. Dinah told them that Clockwork Mouse had bought one yesterday. He was in the cafe eating ice-cream.

"Where's your new bell?" asked Tessie.

"Oh, Gobbo, the goblin, gave me sixpence for it and I bought an ice-cream instead," said Clockwork Mouse.

That night, Noddy tied up his bell so it couldn't ring and he and Tessie crept around the dark town. They were sure Gobbo would break into another house. Suddenly they heard a bell going jingle, jingle. Noddy ran over to Pink Cat's house. Just as he got there, he was knocked over by someone jumping on top of him!

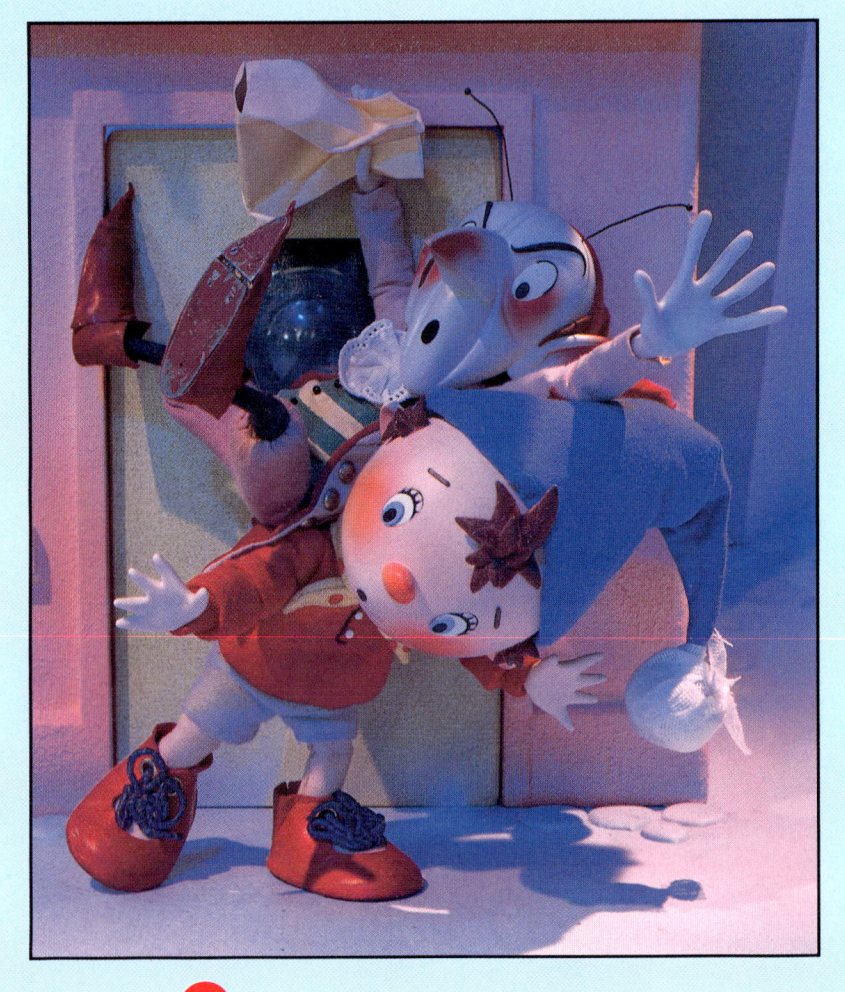

There, with a bell jingling on his hat, was Gobbo! Tessie came running up and picked up a bag of apples and buns that he had stolen. "You bad goblin," she said. "Fancy stealing things and trying to get Noddy blamed for it!"

At that moment, Big-Ears arrived. When he heard what had happened he was very angry indeed.

Gobbo was dragged off to Mr Plod and put into prison. The toys were very upset when they found out that they had wrongly blamed Noddy for being the thief. They all wanted to talk to him and go for a ride with him.

"You'll have to walk today," said Big-Ears. "Noddy is taking Tessie and me for a lovely picnic!"

Toy Town School
with Miss Prim

Learn about sounds

Something to know

In the story 'Noddy and his Bell', Sally hears the bell by using her ears. The piece of your ear on the side of your head is only part of it. There are lots more parts inside your head. The piece on the outside of your head collects the sounds and sends them into your head. The sounds travel to your brain which works out what they mean.

Something to understand

Throw a pebble into a big puddle and watch the ripples spreading across the water. Sound travels through the air and through solid things in the same way. Shout as loudly as you can. Mum will be able to hear the sound through the wall or the floor!

Perhaps you have been in the hills and have heard the echo of your shout. The sound travels across the valley, bounces off the hill and comes back to you. See if you can make your voice echo when you are next out in a hilly place.

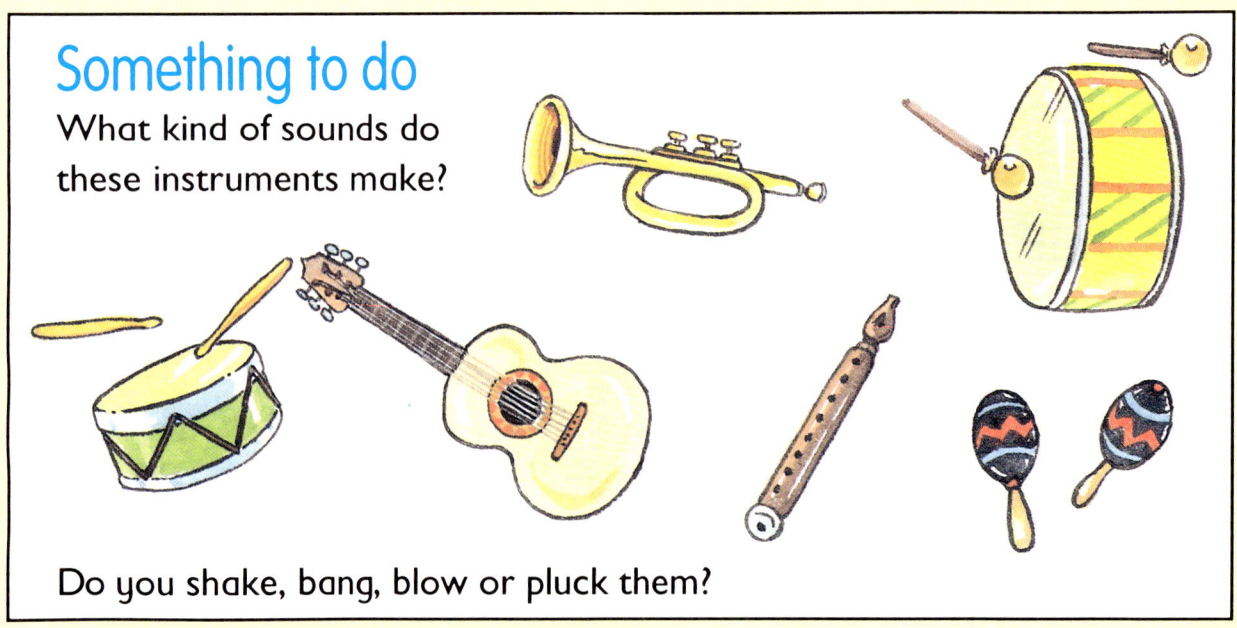

Something to do

What kind of sounds do these instruments make?

Do you shake, bang, blow or pluck them?

The bell on Noddy's hat makes a tinkling sound. The bells in a church tower make a much deeper sound. In London there is a tower with a bell in it called Big Ben. The bell is very heavy and can be heard every hour. Bells are often rung for a special event such as a wedding or on Christmas Day.

MISS PRIM'S NOTE FOR GROWN-UPS

Sound is part of the Science National Curriculum. Talk to your child about different sounds. Go on a walk with them and see what sounds they can hear. Get them to try making different shakers using buttons or seeds instead of rice or peas. Listen to some different types of music. See if they can hear the different sounds.

Something to make

You will need
two clean yogurt pots
some rice or dried peas
sticky tape

Pour a few grains of rice or peas into one of the pots. Stick the two pots together with tape. See what kind of sounds you can make.

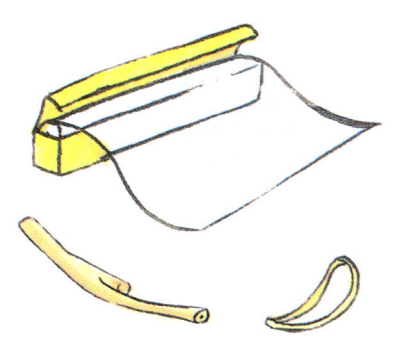

You will need
cling-film
plastic bowl
rubber band
stick

Ask a grown up to cover the bowl with the cling-film. Fix it on with the rubber band. Make sure that the cling-film is tight. Bang the cling-film with the stick. Try a spoon. Does it make a difference?

Learn to Read with NODDY

Dear [tubby bear],

One [rain cloud] day, I borrowed [Big-Ears] [umbrella].
I parked my [car] and went to the grocer's to buy some [jam]. I put down the [umbrella] and took out my [purse]. My [coins] fell out and I could not find it anywhere. I took the [umbrella] and went outside. There was [Mr Plod]. He took the [umbrella] and put it up. And what a surprise, all my [coins] fell out!

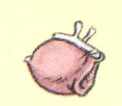

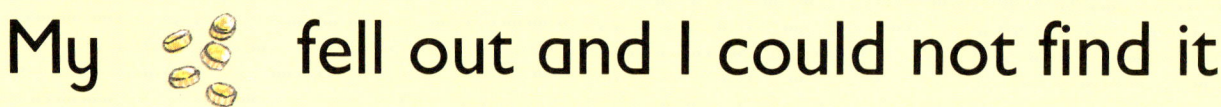

With lots of love from
NODDY

Spot the difference

Noddy has baked a cake and invited Martha Monkey for lunch. The two pictures are not quite the same. Have a close look at both pictures – there are five differences in picture 2 for you to spot.

ANSWERS: 1 Martha's tail is missing. 2 The teapot is a different colour. 3 The cake is missing. 4 The curtains are a different colour. 5 A sandwich is missing.

Noddy Goes to a Party

1 "I have lost my way!" said Noddy. "There is a signpost!"

2 It said 'This Way' and 'That Way', so it was not much help!

3 Noddy drove on – and dear me, he came into *our* land!

4 He heard some children laughing in a house. He stopped.

5 He asked his way. How lovely! They're having a fancy dress party!

6 "Oh, look – here is someone dressed as Noddy!" said a boy.

7 "Hello! Come and play with us, we are having lots of fun!"

8 Now look – Noddy wins the prize for the best fancy dress!

9 "I am *not* in fancy dress!" he says, and how he laughs!

Toy Town School
with Miss Prim

Learn about cooking

Something to know

Parties are fun. You ask friends to share your birthday, Christmas, a wedding or some other special day. Often you will have a special cake to eat. Birthday cakes have candles on them. Easter cakes may have marzipan inside them.

Something to understand

Heating things can change the way they look and feel. An egg is soft and runny before it is cooked, but after it has been cooked, it becomes white and hard. If chocolate is heated, it becomes soft and runny, but when it cools, it turns hard.

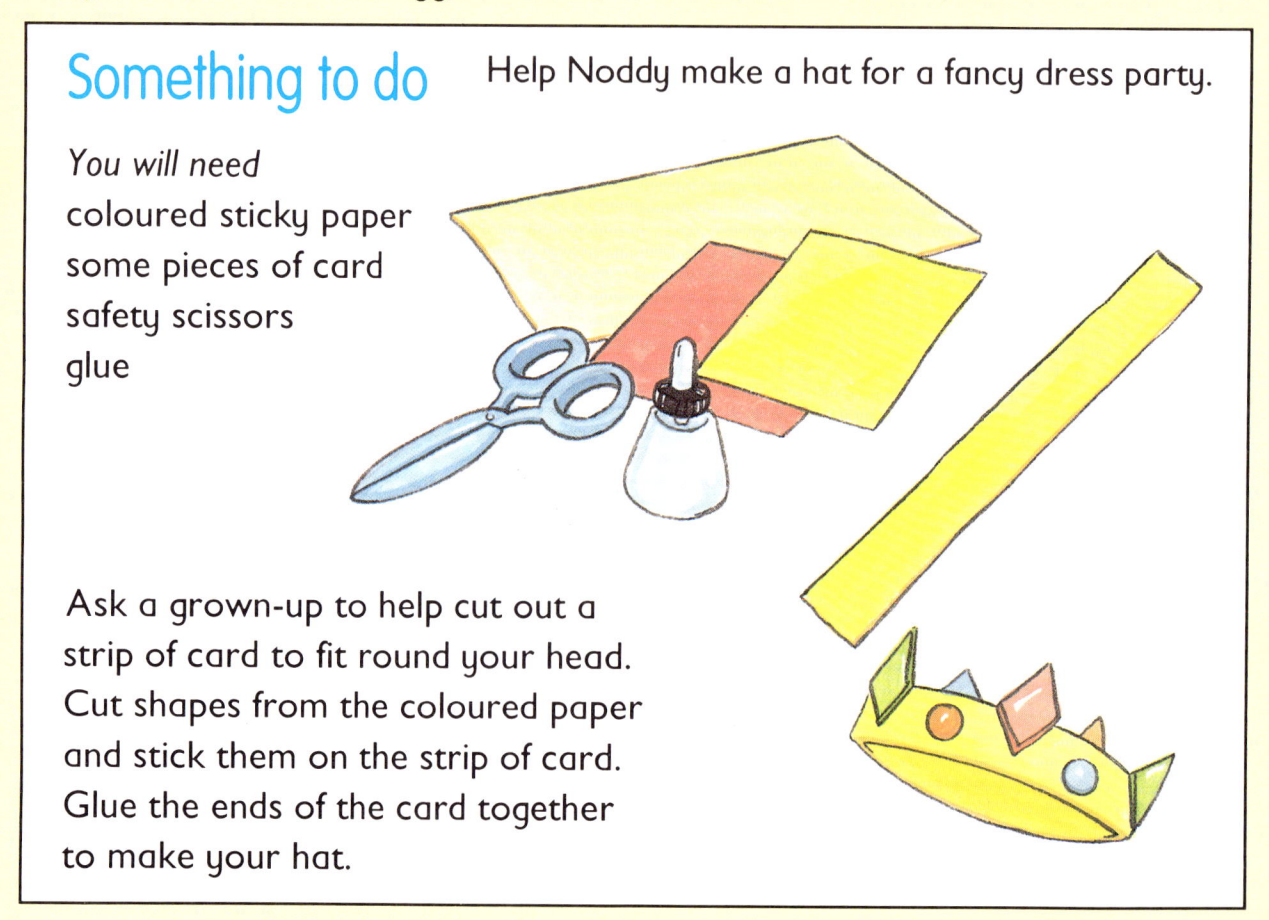

Something to do

Help Noddy make a hat for a fancy dress party.

You will need
coloured sticky paper
some pieces of card
safety scissors
glue

Ask a grown-up to help cut out a strip of card to fit round your head. Cut shapes from the coloured paper and stick them on the strip of card. Glue the ends of the card together to make your hat.

Some things to make

Here are some tasty things that Noddy and his friends have made for their parties.

MISS PRIM'S NOTE FOR GROWN-UPS

There are two safe recipes on this page. Cooking is an important part of the Science Curriculum. Recipes help children with weighing and measurement. Making the hat will give children a chance to try out different designs and patterns. See if there are any ways they can improve on their design.

Noddy's Stuffed Tomatoes

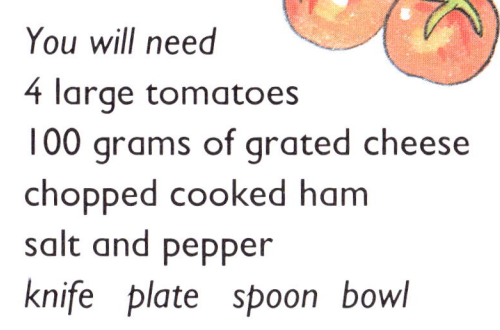

You will need
4 large tomatoes
100 grams of grated cheese
chopped cooked ham
salt and pepper
knife   plate   spoon   bowl

Wash the tomatoes and ask a grown-up to cut off the tops. Take out the insides. Mix up the cheese and ham in the bowl with a little salt and pepper. Fill the inside of the tomato with the mixture. Put on the top. Noddy likes to try other fillings as well.

Pink Cat's Peach and Banana Surprise

You will need
2 bananas
a scoop of ice-cream
4 peach halves
1 level tablespoon of sugar
*bowl   spoon   fork   tablespoon
dessert bowls*

Put the 4 peach halves into 4 dessert bowls. Mash up the 2 bananas in the bowl with a fork and add the sugar. Put a spoonful of mashed banana in each peach half. Add a spoonful of ice-cream on top of the banana.

Remember!
- Be careful with knives.
- Always make sure a grown-up helps you.

After the Party

One night Noddy went to a party at the Noah's Ark with little Tessie Bear. It was a very dark night, so he drove carefully, his bright headlights showing him the road.

"We're nearly there, Tessie," he said. "Look, you can see the Noah's Ark, all lit up!" So it was and very fine it looked, too. Mrs Noah was at the door of the Ark to welcome Noddy and Tessie, and soon they were all having a lovely time with the animals.

First they played 'Here we come gathering nuts in May', and one of the elephants was chosen to pull against one of the lions – so it really was a tussle. The elephant won, of course, though as he pulled with his trunk it was a good deal longer when he had finished pulling, than when he had begun!

Then they played musical chairs and Tessie won that, because Noddy quickly pushed her into the last seat instead of sitting on it himself.

There was a wonderful supper and there were crackers to pull and funny hats to wear. Noddy had a soldier's helmet and felt very grand indeed. He put his own blue hat into his pocket.

Tessie had a witch's hat and that made Noddy laugh. "You'll never look bad enough to be a witch!" he said.

They were all sorry when the party was over and it was time to go. They said good-bye to Mrs Noah, and thank you, and then out of the Ark door everyone went.

"Come on, Tessie," said Noddy. "Let's find the car. Get in and I'll take you home."

He held open the car-door for her and in she got. Noddy slipped into the driving seat, and away they went. It really was a very dark night, so he went rather slowly.

He went round a corner and hooted. "Ooop-ooop-ooop!" Tessie looked at him in surprise.

"What a funny noise your hooter made," she said. "It usually says 'parp-parp' in a sort of high little voice. But that time it said 'ooop-ooop' in a very deep voice."

"Yes. That was odd," said Noddy, surprised, and sounded the hooter again.

And again the car said "ooop-ooop-ooop," in a deep voice.

"What can have happened?" wondered Noddy. "Do you think it's caught a cold, Tessie, and lost its proper voice? It always says 'parp-parp!' I don't like its 'ooop-ooop'."

"*I* think somebody's taken your hooter and given you another," said Tessie. "And Noddy, the cushion I was sitting on when we went to the Ark, has gone. I'm not sitting on one – and it was your very best cushion, wasn't it?"

"Yes. It was," said Noddy. "I always keep it for you to sit on when you wear a nice dress to a party, Tessie. Someone's stolen it – and given me an 'ooop-ooop' hooter!"

"Let's go and tell Mr Plod," said Tessie.

So off they went to the police station and ran inside to tell Mr Plod. But he wasn't there. What a nuisance!

They went outside again – and oh, what a shock they had!

Someone was sitting in the car – they couldn't see who it was, because it was so dark.

"Hey!" cried Noddy. "That's my car!" and he ran over to it.

"Ooop-ooop-ooop!" said the car, and off it went down the street. The person in it shouted something very strange.

"Aha!" he cried, "now I know who stole my car! A witch and a soldier! I'm off to tell Mr Plod." And away went the car round a corner.

"Well! Did you hear *that*?" said Noddy, nodding the helmet he still had on his head. "He's taken our car – and he called us a soldier and a witch."

"Well – you're wearing a helmet that you had at the party and I've got on a witch's hat," said Tessie. "But oh, Noddy – what are we to do? He's taken your car!"

"We'll have to walk," said Noddy, feeling very upset. "Oh, don't cry, Tessie. We'll get my car back all right. I'll take you home and then I'll come back to the police station and see if Mr Plod is there then. Come along."

So up the road they walked, Tessie's paw in Noddy's hand. They turned round the corner – and bumped straight into someone big and solid. "Now, now!" said a voice they knew, and a lamp was flashed over them. It was Mr Plod the policeman!

"Oh, please, Mr Plod," began Noddy – but to his surprise Mr Plod clutched hold of him and Tessie.

"Aha!" said Mr Plod, "so I've caught the soldier and the witch who went off with Mr Whiskers Cat's car! What do you mean by it? You come along with me! Mr Whiskers Cat stopped me in the street just now and told me that his car had been stolen from outside the Noah's Ark – and that he had found it in the street just here, with you two! 'A soldier and a witch'," he said. "So it *must* be you!"

"But I'm little Noddy!" said Noddy, "and this is Tessie Bear."

"Noddy wears a blue cap with a bell and Tessie Bear wears a bonnet," said Mr Plod, taking them along to the police station. But, of course, when they got there and stood under the light, Mr Plod saw quite well that it really was Noddy and Tessie. He *was* most astonished.

"Why did you steal Mr Whiskers Cat's car?" he asked, sternly. "What's happened to yours?"

"Mr Whiskers Cat stole *my* car!" said Noddy, in a rage. "We jumped into my car at the Ark and because the hooter had been changed and my cushion had been stolen we came here to report it to you, Mr Plod. And then suddenly Mr Whiskers Cat yelled at us, jumped into my car and drove off!"

"But it was *his* car. I saw it," said Mr Plod.

And then from outside the door came a curious little noise. "Parp-parp-parp! Parp-parp-parp!" Noddy rushed to open the door at once and Mr Plod shone his torch on to a little car standing patiently beside the pavement – a red and yellow car that said "Parp-parp-parp!" in a polite little voice, so as not to wake anyone up in the houses around.

"Oh, it's my car!" said Noddy,

in surprise. "Did Mr Whiskers Cat bring it back? Its hooter is all right again – and look, Tessie, there's my cushion on the seat. Ooooh – wait till I see Mr Whiskers Cat."

"Oh, Noddy, we must have got into the *wrong* car at the Noah's Ark – don't you see?" said Tessie. "We took Mr Whiskers Cat's car by mistake. *That's* why the hooter was different and there wasn't a cushion."

"What! *You* took his car, Noddy?" said Mr Plod. "Then you must have done it *on purpose*! You know your own red and yellow car too well to take a blue and white one, like Mr Whiskers Cat's."

"But it was *dark* outside the Ark, Mr Plod – so dark that we really didn't see it was a different car," said Tessie Bear, putting her little paw into Mr Plod's big hand. "Please, we're very sorry. Please, Mr Plod."

"All right Tessie Bear," said Mr Plod, gruffly. "I'll let Noddy off this time. Stealing other people's cars and racing round wearing a soldier's helmet and you in a witch's hat. Now go before I change my mind!"

So Noddy and Tessie jumped quickly into the little red and

yellow car and drove off. "Parp-parp!" said the car, pleased to have Noddy driving it again, and not that cross Mr Whiskers Cat, who drove *much* too fast!

"I'll take you home, Tessie," said Noddy, in a small voice. "I'm so sorry I've been silly. Tomorrow I'll go and tell Mr Whiskers Cat I'm sorry I made such a stupid mistake."

So he did, hoping that Mr Whiskers Cat would not be too cross with him. But he wasn't. He laughed and laughed and laughed, and then he and Noddy went off to fetch little Tessie Bear and take her to have an ice-cream with them. "But I don't think we'll ask Mr Plod to join us today," he said, and Noddy agreed with him!

Noddy Says!

- Why did Noddy and Tessie Bear go to see Mr Plod?
- Who did Mr Plod think Noddy and Tessie Bear were?
- Why did Noddy and Tessie Bear get into the wrong car?
- What were the differences between Noddy's car and Mr Whiskers Cat's car?

Hide-and-seek

Everyone is having fun playing hide-and-seek.
Can you help Noddy find all his friends who are hiding?

Toy Town School
with Miss Prim

Something to know

When Noddy and Tessie Bear come out of the party it is very dark and so they get into the wrong car. In towns and villages and on main roads there are street lights so that we can see where we are going. In the country, drivers use their car headlights to see where they are going. People walking along the road often use a torch so that they can find their way.

Learn about making mistakes

MISS PRIM'S NOTE FOR GROWN-UPS

It is important to talk to your child about light and dark. Let them try making some shadow shapes using their hands and the torch. Light is part of the Science National Curriculum. Discuss with them how sometimes we all make mistakes. Finding the odd car out is an exercise in matching and sorting. Get a box of buttons and ask your child to sort them into colour and then shape. Can they see any that do not fit into a group?

Something to try

You will need
a torch
card shapes eg square, circle

In the story 'After the Party', Mr Plod has to shine his torch so that he can see the car. Hold the circle near the torch. Watch what happens to the shadow when you move the circle away from the torch. Now move the torch instead of the card. Try the square.

Something to understand

Sometimes we make a mistake. If we do it is important that we tell someone such as our mum, dad or teacher so that they can put it right. In the story, Mr Plod lets Noddy and Tessie Bear off because they have made a mistake. I don't think he would have been so pleased if they had done it on purpose.

Think of times when you made a mistake. Who helped you sort it out?

Something to do

Tessie Bear and Noddy take the wrong car by mistake.
Look at the cars below. Draw a circle around the odd one out.

Colour them in.

Colour in with Noddy

Noddy and Tessie Bear love ice-cream.

Lucky Little Noddy

"Oh, I do feel so happy tonight, tonight,
For I AM so lucky, you see,
I've a dear little house, and a garage too,
And friends that are fond of me.

I've a beautiful car
    with a loud parp-parp,
And PLENTY of room inside
To take all the people
    who live in Toy Town
Wherever they want to ride.

I love Mrs Tubby, and Tessie Bear too,
And Big-Ears, my Very Best Friend,
I'm really so happy I might sing all night
But I think my song's come to an end!"

COMPETITION

56 SUPER PRIZES TO BE WON!

FIRST PRIZE:
One 44cm NODDY DOLL from Golden Bear

NEXT 5 PRIZE WINNERS EACH RECEIVE:
One 22cm NODDY DOLL from Golden Bear

NEXT 20 PRIZE WINNERS EACH RECEIVE:
One NODDY or BIG-EARS HAND PUPPET from Golden Bear

30 RUNNER UP PRIZES from Michael Stanfield

10 Thirty-piece Wooden Jigsaws
10 Big Shaped Puzzles 
10 Twelve-piece Shaped Puzzles 

Michael Stanfield toys and games are available at all major toy shops and superstores.

HOW TO ENTER

It's easy! All you have to do is answer this simple question:

What is on the end of Noddy's hat?

Write the answer on a postcard or envelope, with your name, age and address.

Send to:
Noddy Competition, Marketing Department, Egmont Publishing, PO Box III, Great Ducie Street, Manchester M60 3BL.

Closing date: 1st February 1996.

The first 56 correct entries selected at random after the closing date will win a prize.

RULES
Employees of World International or their respective agents may not enter this competition. The Editor's decision is final and no correspondence will be entered into. A list of winners' names will be available on request and on receipt of a SAE after 14th February 1996. The Publishers reserve the right to vary the prizes, subject to availability at the time of judging the competition.